Chiapas Diary

poems by

Elaine R. Chamberlain

Finishing Line Press
Georgetown, Kentucky

Chiapas Diary

ACKNOWLEDGMENTS

I want to thank my daughter-in-law Sara Ries-Dziekonski for her help in
preparing this Chapbook.

Publisher: Leah Huete de Maines
Editor: Christen Kincaid
Cover Art: Photo by Ted Dziekonski
Author Photo: Ted Dziekonski
Cover Design: Elizabeth Maines McCleavy

Order online: www.finishinglinepress.com
also available on amazon.com

Author inquiries and mail orders:
Finishing Line Press
PO Box 1626
Georgetown, Kentucky 40324
USA

Table of Contents

The Highlands

Clouds
pour down from heaven
dropping their silken hair.
Clouds
Bleed up the mountain
dampening her thighs.
Clouds
play a blue song
on a slow flute.

The roads wind up and around
and through a quilt
of cane and corn and coffee.
The feet of the shepherdess quicken.
She gathers her flock and disappears.

Trees
are spectators.
Observers
in silver and silence.

Trees
are tall women
with gracious arms.

I did not know
I would look down
from a mountain
and weep with the joy of trees.

I did not know I would ever
see into the peace of trees:
that there are cloudy places
where trees
sway
like ships
on a sea.

I did not know
I could love a valley
and a mountain
as much as I have loved
a man
and a child.

The Cristobal Colon Bus

I.

Polished but peeling old but not dead wheezing, panting
smoking, farting
the Cristobal Colon bus with a face full of dents the body broken
the rear hopelessly crumpled,
is a vehicle of dream and despair. The doors will not close.
The windows will not open.
And the brakes are hardly there.

But if you ride
with carbon monoxide long enough
it becomes your friend. You begin to like
the smell of it—
you and the chickens and the very sleepy turkeys.

II.

The driver's windshield is a shrine to the night.
A red green white twinkling of Christmas lights.
Twelve Mexican flags flutter on twelve trembling toothpicks.
The Virgin of Guadalupe in a blue velvet robe
is blinking her glass bead eyes twisting jerking jiggling
her wire spring neck nodding her plastic head.

Round and around the curves
we go phosphorescent
rosaries swinging.
It's a game of crack the whip.

Above the rearview mirror a sign in colored glass
backed with aluminum foil: hand lettered:
Jesus Cristo mi Senor
protect the driver por favor!

The Epiphany

It was on the Cristobol Colon bus
heading through the mountains
late at night, tropical storms
jetting the windows.

The driver bent his head toward
the mountains his radio
on low and wound
round the curves like a dancer:
Left right
Left right
    Left.

        Pulling.
          Swerving.
            Dancing a Cha-Cha-Cha
      for flashing fools
    who passed by fast
    saying their foolish rosaries.

        At the rear of the bus
        lovers in darkness
        young, sensuous
        spongy with hormones.
        They clenched and fondled
        like eager octopi

        while we
        in the midsection
        sober and somber
        grimy with sweat
        rocked to the
        uneasy rhythms of the storm.

The wipers pulsed
irritably
erratically
with tachycardic nervousness
with hypertensive fret.
Set high.
Set low.
Set high.

And the rain was not rain
but an evacuation
of rock, root, and tree.

And the road was not a road
but a moonscape.
A dark pox.
A skin of eroding craters.
A road digesting itself.

And my brain rode the road
with only one question.
How would my family find me?

I saw myself
heading north
by slow train
in a coffin
of chipped ice.

Then the lightning
began
and I moved forward.
Better to glimpse
that fast ballet
of splendid
luminous mountains.

And as the mountains revealed themselves
I learned that an epiphany
comes only once
but remains
on the mind
like a ghost.

The Altamirano

Dog barks.
A second answers.
Grand chorus of dogs now.

Cacophany of crows.
Hum of crickets.
Running sandaled feet.

Corridas on the radio.
A tin whistle. A clay drum.
"Radio Chiapas! Diez y ocho horas por dia!"

Whoosh of water in a wooden trough.
A young man washing his shirt.
Singing his heart out.

Laughter in a dirt play yard.
Little boys twisting on a yellow rope swing.
Slap of tortillas on a clay comal.

Staccatoed cheep of baby chicks.
Clop of burro hooves.
Whir of bicycle tires.

Cackle of hens.
Girls selling muffins.
Scrape of breakfast chairs.

Hobbled hop of horses.
Pick axe. Machete.
A diesel relieving itself.

Hummingbirds in the florepondia.
A grapefruit falls from the grapefruit tree.
Esther calling my name.

Assessing Manuel

I.   Head

Hair comes out in
clumps. Combs like
raking grass.

Skin falls off
in patches.

Eyes
half-opened
will train on objects.

Lifting the lashes is effort.
Pupils reactive.

  Airway
  Patent.

Mouth. A chapped
oval of impetigo.

  Mouth
  an ovular
  soundless
  cry.

Will wave head if food is offered.

II.   Chest and Arms

There are rattles. There are rales.
There's a slow
growl
in the lungs.

  The heart is a muscle.
  The heart is a pump.
  The heart is a panting animal.
  The heart is hiding.
  The heart is playing dead.
  The heart is playing statue
in the chest.
The pulse is a magician
is a trickster is a rabbit.
The pulse can turn on.
The pulse can turn off.
Disappear.

Wait!

The pulse is sweet
is candy is syrup.
The pulse is reaching

the thin thread stage
the soft ball stage.
The pulse is hardening.

The arms are sticks.
Little human Pick Up Sticks.
Lift them.
They fall.
Again.
Again.

III.   Extremities

Strange
how the nails
have darkened have bruised.
As if a door
had been shut on them.

And the legs
in circumference
are larger at the ankles than at the thighs.

And the legs
turn in at the knees and bow
as if hunger
were a horse
to be ridden.

Memorial

I was the one
who prepared the child
filing his tiny openings
closing his wide dark eyes.
The lashes shadowed his cheeks
with dark embroidery.

I tore a sheet
cut a suit
slipped in
cold head
cold arms
cold feet.

I took the remaining cloth
and wound it round
and gave the bundle
to his mother

who placed it
before an altar
and lit a fire
of copal.

One by one
we burned
the bitter
leaves of Eucalyptus.

La Mama

She lies on the ground on a feed sack.
Her naked twins lie on another.
One stillborn; the other dying.
It is January. Night falls
like a sour shroud.

Her back is to the babies.
Her arms and legs are drawn.
Her abdomen distended.
Her face, a skull.

By her eyes
you know she is listening.

To the bleating of flocks slaughtered by soldiers.
Two husbands locked in the church.
Tortured. Disappeared.

To the scuffle of her sister.
Dancing her last jarabe tapetio.
A plastic bag taped to her head.

  How much can you hear
  before you hear nothing?

She is listening
to her naked ones
placed cold upon the ground.

She hears the creatura live
laboring for breath.
She hears the creatura lost
wending its way over mountains.

How much can you hear
before you hear nothing?

Sor Isa's Orchids

Sor Isa can't resist a certain orchid
dog-faced, yellow butterfly flecked.

She can't resist
the waxy weight of it. the sensual flesh

sweet-scented
like the hands of a child

like the imagined love of a man.

In sandals
she is trudging through the forest to the river
where yellow orchids grow

past soldiers and shadows and trees no longer blooming
and grass no longer green.

She runs past the bones of the disappeared
past the teeth of the disappeared
past the place where the ground is weeping.

She remembers to remember only the living.

She loosens her sandals
and climbs the tree
where orchids grow.

In her mind she can see the flowers on her altar

beside her row of miniature huts
reminders of the hovels of the poor.

They will grow as orchids do.
On air. On grace.
They will fill her room
with the scent of survival.

Bathing in the Lacandon Forest

The Sacumilja leaps and falls staggers and crashes
cursing and snorting
like a great drunken fool.

It would be better to bathe in the Mendosa
where calmer, broader waters
deposit a load of agate and loam.
But the nun has spotted a fisherman.

For her modesty
we must go deeper into the forest
cross a railess bridge, hike the Sacumilja
chain up and feel for tenuous footing.

She is the first to remove her clothing.
Hanging her wimple on a bamboo.
Placing one sandal here. Another there.
Shaking out her glossy hair.

Curious but embarrassed, we look
away. When we turn back she is pulling
off her underthings and slipping into
an icy pool.

She takes a long time slicking down her hair
sudsing it up again
sweeping it in and out of the water.

Now the Tzeltal women are naked to the waist and they wade in,
water dragging their indigo skirts.

Two iridescent papilios
flash and hang like fragile joy
above the disappearing trees.
Seven kilometers away
government earth movers
snort and scrape a road which
will one day connect
the forest to a brave new world.
For now that world remains apart:

a distant rumbling. Like something not well digested.
Like something misunderstood.

Alfredo's Business

Alfredo was doing well
driving supply truck for the nuns.
He built a tiny house across from the hospital.
Two rooms cement floor adobe walls tin roof
electric lights gas refrigerator a two tank propane stove.
When the link to the highway came he built an addition
and turned the front of his house into a general store.

He had shelves on three sides. A little of everything.
Two pound packs of animal crackers. Boxes of shortbread from Seville.
Cornflakes. Twinkies. Bimbo bread. Chilies. Toilet paper. Kleenex.

He had Venus Rose soap. Cooking oil in its own bottle.
Or the cheaper kind where you brought your own bottle and Alfredo
poured you some oil from the big drum. He had La Abuelita chocolate
in powder or disc. Instant Atole. And gingham sacks of corn meal and
     flour.
He had coffee rice beans. Soap powder flea powder ammonia and
     bleach.
Bundles of twigs for scouring. Fresh bananas and oranges.
Family sized boxes of gelatin and flan. Baskets of eggs.
Baskets of onions. Limes. Mountains of ripe tomatoes.

He had kaopectate Aspirina Peptobismal
Brylcreem Burma Shave Brut.
Crest Colgate Ultrabrite.
Jergens lotion Johnsons cream.

He had all kinds of shampoo and conditioners.
And Agua de Florida in skinny bottles with floral design.

He had an ice box by the door
with a reservoir of cool water
where floated Coca Pepsi Sidral.
He had a red rag for wiping their tops.

Alfredo's best box was reserved for fruit ices
which his wife made from overly ripe bananas and limes.

There was a clear plastic case for Chiclets.
And a large glass jar for peppermints.
There were cellophane bags of taffies.
Jelly beans   sourballs   cinnamon suckers.
There were nuts   apricots   raisins   prunes.
There were rat traps and mouse traps.
Insecticides and fungicides. Pine oil for toilets and floors.

There were six different shades of nail polish
and matching lipsticks too. There were colored combs
barrettes   ribbons   brushes   bobby pins   lash curlers   nets.
There were skin bleaches   powders   passionate musky perfumes.

There were squares of muslin
embossed with blue sentiments
to embroider and sew into pillows:

Sleep well my husband. Mother's love.
I'm looking for a sweetheart. Forget me not.

There was a tray of boleos.
And trays of buñuelos.
A tray of sugar cookies.
And a kettle of hot boiled corn.

Then the government built a new hospital.
And the army attacked the old one.
And the air force bombed the fields.
And the soldiers took thirty-seven men
from their houses
to the church
for torture

and only seven
returned.

And the party
offered Alfredo
twice as much
to drive for them.
And he accepted.

We no longer buy Cocas.
Nor fruited ice.
But Alfredo doesn't mind.
Alfredo doesn't need our business.

At the Medical Staff House

Things don't change too fast here.
Electricity is new. Customs are old.
At sundown everyone goes to bed.
Ours is the only house with lights. Neighbors don't like it.
It keeps the chickens awake.

Our house is whitewashed adobe.
The roof, corrugated.
We open the door with a coat hanger.
The latch has been broken for years.

Walk into the house through the kitchen.
Wipe your shoes on the rag at the door.
Ignore the mice. Ignore the sink.
Female doctors do not wash male doctors' dishes.
Neither do nurses. Especially Reina.

Reina gives the dentist a foot massage. Then he rubs her back.
They like to impress one another with Freudian comments.
(Doctors still believe in Freud.)

Reina rejects all theories. She believes in smoking
writing letters and crossword puzzles.
She's been on call.
It takes four nights to unwind.

The internist and the anesthesiologist drink wine in their room.
The anesthesiologist gets high and reads *Indiana Jones*.
The internist stays sober and reads articles on spastic colon
and paralytic ileus. He suspects he may have ascarides and is
developing a bowel obstruction.

He's from France. Charrola land.
Home of the famous cattle. The anesthesiologist says charrolas
come from Texas. (He's from Texas.) They argue in the rain.

It's been raining for three months.
Rain brings ecological redistribution.
Wildlife moves inside.
When we shower, giant cockroaches drop on our shoulders.
Furry spiders scuttle under our couch.
A mama spider with babies on her back
escapes high water out by the laundry tubs.

The other nurse has a spider phobia.
She sleeps under a net and is often away.
She has a boyfriend in the Ocosingo.
If the rains continue she may marry him.

Termites are chewing the ceiling.
Dropping digested wood on our beds.
One of these days the ceiling will collapse and
we'll be introduced to the rat family that scampers overhead.

Jaime the surgeon is showering and singing La Boheme.
Afterward he will strut like a rooster.
I cannot bear it.
In my mind I make maps of whatever he touches
of where his soap has been
and of the positions of his comb.
One gray curl rests
on the windowsill.

At dawn the sky flames.
Low clouds flutter and rustle. Mists dance like muted birds.
A tarantula graces the banana tree with her kaleidoscope of silver.
Sontsotles sing of water. Of priceless simple things:
A damp horse with thick fur
feeding in the courtyard.
Dew on a comb.
The grace of one curl.

Aurelianna

She refused to eat.
And lay there like a stone.
The beans I fed her rolled down her chin.
I could not make her swallow.

I bribed her with Chiclets
barrettes and a Teddy bear.
She took my gifts.
And pushed away my soup.

I washed her face and
braided her hair.

I wanted her to live so much I let her die.
And loved her so much I hated her.

Huertas Delicias

I.

In this blurred Cuernavaca photo
you and I were extraordinarily young.
Your beard was red.
Your waist was a boy's.
And my legs were strong horses.

We were green as the grass we postured in.
Poinsettias bloomed like pelicans,
like flamingos, like storks.
The mispero delivered her fruit.
Remember it.

This other photo is unclear.
Valerie took this.
There is her finger;
a blotch in the corner.
She refuses to develop.

Valerie.
Chestnut hair.
The color of nothing
in the tropics.

II.

I believed in happiness
and it was misery
beneath the grace of volcanoes.
Popocatepetl
lay beside our window
delicious and unreachable;
more feminine than legend
and perfectly asleep.

At noon, Brahman cattle
lumbered up the hill
to feed in a hot palm shed.
At noon, where everything is fed.

The sidewalk shoe man took his rest
under speckled bougainvillea
and a caged centzontle sang.

The milkman clattered home
under a mountain of cans
steaming tortillas
balanced on his hand.

The horse was roan,
almost the color
of Valerie's hair.

III.

The milkman
offered his horse.
I wanted to buy it,
believing beauty was for sale.

Happiness was owning
and so I never knew it
when it lit upon the palms,
when it clattered with the birds.

I could not feel it
as it curled like a cat
in the unused, outdoor oven.
I ignored its swaying
in the genital, green papayas.

I did not recognize its scent
in the narcotic flor de nardo.
Bitterness lay beside me
and grew.
Like a child
with wild
persimmon hair.

Feeding Mariano

Day One:
Ignore the dry skin
the bones poking through it the bony arms, the bony legs
the phantom movements of the ribs the beads of his spine
slipping through your fingers.

Ignore the ghostly breath. Anchor the head.
Concentrate on the mouth. When he wails, be ready.
Pop in whatever.
Just be quick.
When he thrusts it out thrust it in again.
When he cries pop in more.

Day Two:
Find his weakness the food he has not quite
given up. Bananas? Chicken?

Make a pulp. Anchor the head. Pop in chicken. Pop in bananas.
Let him cry. Pop in more.

Day Three:
Notice the eyes. Their teary brightness.
Yesterday they were dry.
Notice the butterfly lightness of his hand
on your cheek.
See his little leg. How it swings in your lap
like the clapper of a bell?

Notice the beating of his temple.
How tenuous,
and hopeful.

Jaime

I have decided at my age
and after too many husbands that love is
impossible.

Therefore
I will not learn your gorgeous language nor look romantically
into your large romantic eyes.
As you move from table to shower
I will not observe your slender waist nor the down
on your arm.

When I think of your hands
I'll think of rubber gloves stretched over them.
And see the hands of a thief.

I will remember the diabetic foot you debrided
as ruthlessly as I tore apart
last November's turkey.

I will remember
the relentless mountain of stinky teeth
you pulled from an old man's mouth.

And when you sing Cuban love songs I'll remember you
sewing stretched skin over a tattered, ruined abdomen

after removing a green appendix.

This is how I survive
sharing a house with a man

with the eyes of a saint
the waist of a David
and the voice of Pavarotti.

Margarita

Margarita wanted to live. She was wide awake
when they brought her in.
The surgeon was nervous. His radio played Wagner.
No one thought to turn it down.

We were caught in our own little cages of anxiety.
Margarita lay nude beneath the sheet.
Her fingers clawed to the cotton.

Before she was completely under the surgeon taped her eyes
extended the table and strapped her down.
Thin, hypoxic she struggled and then let go.

He dug in her gut one hour, two three.
searching for the part of her intestine
which the government doctors lost.

The anesthesiologist used all he had
to keep her flying.
His mountain of bottles grew and grew
as Margarita went down and down.

Even Sor Juana under
the crucifix shouting   panicky

could not stop Margarita.

Three blue hot water bottles placed on her trunk
could not warm her.

Her skin turned ash.

And her pulse disappeared.
But I thought
I could feel it.
I can feel it now

Seven Points

Eat a big plateful of beans every day.
Diarrhea is good for you.
It cleans the pipes.

On your way to anywhere say hello to everyone.
When passing a large group don't be stingy.
Use more than one hello. Divide and distribute them.
The more the better.
Buenas dias—ten times ten times ten.

Expect screw ups.
They will come.
You'll get used to them. So will your friends.
And they'll maintain a straight face when you ask
for the use of a penis and you really mean to say,
"May I borrow your comb?"

Slow down.
Getting the job done is not important.
Laughing, clowning, touching is.
Awaken late.
Stretch. Yawn. Scratch.
Take long showers.
Take an hour over lunch.
Take an hour over dinner. Sing

Cry when you sing.
Laugh when you cry. Dance.
Walk in the night of a thousand stars.
Walk in the garden of endless delight.
Observe how silver runs down the papaya.
How the calabasa curls.
How naked children
have built a dam
of mud and stones.

When the sun comes out
so will the flies.
Catch them between the curtains
and the glass.
Pop them.
Flies can be fun.
If there are many open the door.
 Herd them out like horses.

Take a rest on your bed
with your shoes on.
Listen to the dry corn singing in the milpa.
Remember in Altamirano
even corn has learned to sing.

Elaine Chamberlain grew up in Seattle. She has lived in Mexico and later did volunteer work in the Hospital San Carlos in a remote village in Chiapas, Mexico. She graduated from the University of Buffalo. Her mentors were John Logan and Robert Creeley.

She has retired from three careers: teaching art and literature; nursing; and mental health counselling. Elaine loves to travel. She has made several trips to India, has gone by chicken bus through Central and South America, and once travelled by boat down the Amazon where she fell in love with a tree sloth.

Elaine is the former area coordinator of the New York State Poets in the Schools program, and a founding member of Earth's Daughters. She taught Creative Writing and Composition at Erie Community College. Her poems have appeared in several venues including the *Buffalo News, Friends Journal, Sow's Ears*, and the collection *A Celebration of Western New York Poets*. Her first book of poetry *Pictures from the Bee House*, was published by White Pine Press.

Elaine now lives in Hamburg, New York with her husband Ted Dziekonski and two yappy Chihuahuas. She makes dioramas in her spare time. In fact, her living room is so full of dioramas that it is hard to find a place to walk. The space that isn't taken up by dioramas is crammed with indoor trees. Elaine is a gardener as well. In early spring the front yard is a maze of tulips and daffodils.

www.ingramcontent.com/pod-product-compliance
Lightning Source LLC
LaVergne TN
LVHW041329080426
835513LV00008B/642